CW00520024

Make Art your Business

By Kerri's Fine Arts

This book is dedicated to my long-suffering husband who has had to put up with me, and my many hobbies and all the mess that comes with them yet still supports me all the say, to my children who are always a source of love and encouragement. And to the many artists and friends that have helped to guide me on my journey

-Kerri

Forward

I have loved to create as far back as I can remember, one of my earliest memories is my mum telling people that I could make anything out of paper. Every day, every moment I would make or draw. I never saw this as a possible career, it just wasn't a 'proper' job. Art was for the elite, either that or you would be a starving artist?

I have worked in a variety of sectors since I left school, I have been in and out of the equestrian world since I was 16, it was my love of horses that re-lit my passion for drawing. My children started riding lessons and endless photos followed, as parents we literally take photos of everything they do. These photos sparked my creative juices and I began to draw. I also worked for an amazing businesswoman, Entrepreneur in my younger years. Dawn Gibbons, the founder of a company called Flowcrete, this lady is the embodiment of positive thinking, she taught me that anything is possible if you just believe it. I worked in the marketing department and learned many valuable skills that have out me on the path to start my own business.

I have always felt that there was more to my life than working for someone else, helping them to up their profits, create and market new products. In the latter years I became a childminder so that I could stay home and raise my kids.   What has that got to do with being an artist I hear you say? Well I have to say the time I have spent self-employed has been the most fundamental part of creating a successful art career.

This is where I learned all the valuable skills from time management to bookkeeping and dealing with those lovely tax bills.

Every journey I have been on in my life has led me to this destination, a place where all my dreams are coming true and I want you there too.

Introduction

There comes a time where we know to the core what it is we want to do with our lives, this can happen at any point, it's that drive that pushes you. That near obsession that gets you out of bed every morning to do what you love. For me it was during my mid-life crisis, all my life I have worked jobs that were expected of me. For most people turning their hobby, their passion into a business can feel like a far away dream. I am here to tell you that it is not a dream it is your purpose in life and it can be reality.

To do this you have to really want it; you must turn off your doubts and fears and believe in yourself and your work. If this is what you REALLY want to do then I am here to help you all the way.

Who am I and how can I help you?

I am a middle-aged mum of two teenagers, married with 2 horses, a dog, and a bearded dragon (my inspiration). I have worked in numerous jobs since leaving school, jobs that I did for the money, not for the love just a means to pay the bills. I am sure that many of you have been there or are still there now. But did you know you have a choice? For too many years you hear the words, 'but it won't pay the bills', 'its just a pipe dream.' Well, those words are not useful and will not get you where you want to be. Isn't it time to be wealthy doing something you love?

I am a mixed media artist, I create portraits using acrylics, coloured pencil, and pen. I started drawing professionally 5 years ago, and it wasn't long before I knew that this is what I wanted to do full time. I have been self employed in a different sector for 15 years previously so I was already equipped with the business knowledge to set up as an artist. That is not to say it was an easy road.

This is where I can help you, I have been there and done that as they say, I have tried failed, and tried again, I have learned the hard way how not sell so that you don't have too.

In the following pages I will help you to organise your mindset so that you believe that **you are an artist**, there is no worse critic than ourselves. I will help you with pricing, finding your niche, where and how to sell, creating multiple income streams and moving forward.

If you believe it is your time and you are ready to step up and own your future then turn the page and let's get started.

Keri Rendell

Table of Contents

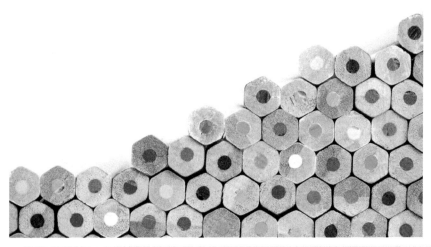

Mindset

How many times have you thrown away a piece of work or posted on social media and received no likes? How many times have you doubted your own work and said to yourself it's not good enough to sell?

Do you really believe that? I give you a challenge go and search around on the internet, in books or galleries and find 2 pieces of artwork that to you are average or at best okay and then find the price tag, do you think they doubted their work? Of course, they did as an artist we are our own worse critics. This is not a bad thing as it means we always strive to improve.

To make it (in your own mind) first have to 'fake it' I don't mean paint copies of other peoples work, what I do mean is fake your belief in yourself? Why? Because we can fool our minds into believing what we say as fact so the first thing you need to do it tell yourself that you are an artist, look in the mirror every morning and tell yourself, 'I AM an artist', if anybody asks what you do you tell them 'I am an artist' it may feel like a lie at the beginning but the more you say it and the more you tell other people the easier it will sit in your mind and you will start to believe it.

"Yes you, you there, you are an artist."

This may all sound a little 'woo woo' to some but heck, if it works why not try it, what do you have to lose. Surround yourself with positive affirmations around your work, reinforcing belief daily will keep you in the correct mindset, do simple things that will remind you of your dream. Set a reminder on your phone or computer that says, 'I am a very wealthy artist' or 'I am living my best life'. Have ornaments, pictures jewellery around that reminds you of what and where you want to be. At all times see yourself as **an artist.**

Be clear in your mind

Take a moment, a piece of paper and a pen. Sit a, no don't start drawing yet. Have a think about what it is you really want to achieve with your art business.

Answer these questions:

Do you want fame and fortune or do you want to make a comfortable living out of the limelight?

How many hours a day do you WANT to create art?

What barriers are in your way?

I want you to write down how you would like your day to go, how much time will you spend creating, do you want to be responsible for every aspect of your business, from creating to packaging, shipping and marketing?

Keep these answers close by you at all times, keep a focus on what you want to achieve, let it influence your daily decisions to get you where you want to be.

Remember you do not need to know everything from the start. You will learn as you go.

How many hours a day do you want to work, how flexible is your time? Do you want to work in the evenings at weekends? There is no right or wrong answer here, this is the joy of working for yourself you set your own hours and schedules. Heck you can even go and create whilst sitting on a beach in Australia if you so choose (careful of the sand in your paints not the best unless you want a very textured finish) What you need to do is get a clear picture in your mind of how you want it to be. This way you can make sure that every step you take is taking you in the right direction to your dream life.

When I started out, I had no idea what I wanted or where I was going, I didn't value my work and I had no boundaries on my time. I was answering messages at midnight, drawing into the early hours to hit deadlines, and accepting all work that came along. This resulted in me feeling drained, overworked underpaid, and rapidly losing the passion that set me on this path in the first place. I soon realised that there was no way I could carry on like this, if I had taken the time to work out my profit margins I was probably working for pennies or worse a negative margin. This wasn't going to enable me to quit my full-time job and live the dream. I was slowly falling into the starving artist mentality.

Something had to change.

One of the hardest things I needed to learn was how to say 'NO', you may think this is a silly way to get business but stay with me here.

Reasons to say NO

It is a fact that not all people appreciate the hard work that goes into creating a piece of art, you will be asked, 'Can you just do me a little picture of my dog/cat/child/car?' and the moment you say. 'Yes, it will be 'x' amount' you will get responses such as, oh I thought you could just do it for free, or oh I didn't think it would be that much. Or worse they will just ghost you.

Very early on you when you are asked for a piece of art you will 'see' a sale, get all excited, then feel deflated when the order isn't placed. Don't take this to heart, a rule of thumb when selling is on average 1%, which means for every 100 interested people you may get 1 sale. This is not just limited to the art sector it applies to all markets, don't despair all you need is eyes on your work to up sales rate.,

What you need to do to save your sanity early on is put into place is an auto response to messages stating your process and most importantly your prices and terms, this way if they are truly interested, they will contact you again, it is at this point that you can start to build up a relationship with your customer. It will save you time and disappointment and stop you having to check your messages every 2 seconds, which then leads to just looking at social media to oh no I've lost an hour where did that go!

My Auto response reads something like this:

-

Hi

Thank you for taking an interest in my commissions/artwork/prints

My prices for these pieces are: £££££

What I require from yourself is …………………

If you are interested in placing an order or booking a place on the waiting list, please follow the link below to place your order.

Once deposit/payment is received I will be in touch to discuss your requirements.

I look forward to working with you.

Kerri

When you first start getting enquiries for orders you will feel the need to fulfil every single one, as though it is your duty, you will say yes to everything which usually results in burnout. What you need to keep clear in your mind as orders com in, is 'Will this keep me on track to achieve my dream?' taking on a commission is ultimately your choice. If the subject is not in your skill set or if the photo/image is not clear then what you will produce will probably not be your 'BEST'.   As an artist you want to exhibit your best work.

So, learning to say no is a fundamental skill to creating longevity in your business. You want customers that are so happy with their piece they tall all their friends, after all word of mouth is the best marketing.

Check out the work of other artists in your niche, what are they displaying, do they show all their work? When you are looking into other artist, following groups etc, don't start to compare your work with theirs, every piece of art is unique to the individual, use other people's work to improve your own but don't decide the value of your ort based on your perception of theirs.

Working from home

It is too easy to let 'other things' get in the way, leading us to believe we can't do it You will probably begin this journey working from home. How nice to be able to be at home with your kids, your pets, your spouse etc   NO...... you are at home to WORK. Make it clear to all that although you are at home you are also at WORK. You need to set aside a space and set time where you are on DO NOT DISTURB. It is so easy to. Just put the washing in, or just tidy this or clean that. Don't fall into this trap if you are going to create a business to support you and your family, you need to treat it like a business. Set your hours and turn up ready to work, and no not in your PJ's. why because you need the mindset that this is your job, your business your career. Would you turn up in your PJs if you worked in a public gallery/studio, I'm sure the majority of us would not unless this is your style of course.

remember Make Art your Business.   Run it as a business. I will show you how.

Please compete the following task, it doesn't take long to do and is so very important in clarifying your goals and keeping you on the path of your desires.

'Imagination is more important than knowledge'

-Albert Einstein

Notes.......

Task 1

Making Art my Business		
What do I want to create?	Original Art	
	Commissions	
How much do I want/need to make?		
What is my ideal customer? Age/income/passions		
How many hours a week do I want to work?		
Where do I want to work? Home/studio		
What affirmations have I put into place?		
When do I want this to happen by?		

Finding your Niche

If you are like me then you may feel you don't need or want a niche you just want to be free to create whatever you please. I am not here to say that you cannot do that, in an average week I can be doing commissions of pets, watercolour abstract or designs on surfboards to creating pieces out of resin or clay. Having a niche doesn't mean losing your creative spark.

What a niche does is give you focus, you will be more inclined to one medium or style than the others in the beginning and this is fantastic, as to become successful and known to you need to stand out from everyone else.

I stated out by doing pencil drawings of my horse, he was the reason I picked up a pencil, from this I was asked to produce drawings for friends and family, the more I did the more I could see my skills Improving. I realised that I loved drawing horses, this progressed to everything hairy

Find that one thing that makes you want to get out of bed to create, what sparks that passion in you?

Who is your inspiration? Have you investigated other artists that are in a similar field to yourself?

Following your idol is a fantastic way to gain insight into what you really want. Go and follow their social media, check out their webpage. What is it that draws you to them, is it their style or their skill? Often, we will look at the work of others and just think. Oh, I will never be that good.

remember you are not looking at their early pieces, you are looking at their established works, the pieces that they chose to put out there.

We all start somewhere, following a more established artist will inspire you to create and improve on your own pieces, it will provide you with ideas and motivate you to keep going. There are many artists online that offer classes whether free on YouTube or paid sites such as Patreon. Trust me when I say subscribing or just scheduling time in your week to dedicate to study is the fastest way to advancing your skills and therefore your business. You should never stop learning; we never know everything. They say to become a master at a given skill takes 10, 000 hours, that is approximately 416 days if you don't eat sleep or leave your easel. Putting in the hours is the only way to guarantee you will improve. Learn to always carry a sketch book with you, there maybe be moments in the day where you have a spare 5 minutes (if we're lucky), just doodle or draw what you see. Every stroke is practice and practice makes perfect.

Having a niche is important because if you try to cater to everyone your overall work won't speak to anyone. Your niche is also be linked to who your ideal client is. So, it's important you have a targeted niche market and speak to a customer or client in a certain way which they can really relate to.

A niche will help you to keep focus, you will become known for what you do, when somebody asks a friend or posts a question on social media forums asking if anybody knows anyone who can do a portrait of her dog for example, if this is your niche people will recall that they will have seen your name and your pictures of dogs. Also, by establishing a niche you will build up a l portfolio of specific subjects that you are able to show as examples.

Target audience

By establishing a niche, you will be able to identify your target market.

If your chosen subject is pets your target market are people who love pets/animals. Join social network groups for pets, dog lovers, cat sites etc. This was you can build up relationships with people that are interested in your work.

Think about your target market, where would you normally find them, what do they like to do in their spare time. How can you get your art where they will see it? We will go more into this in the marketing section. For now, just think about where you can find people interested in your work.

🐘 **Remember:** Your niche does not need to limit your art, keep creating the pieces that you want but for the purpose of starting out in business limit your marketing to your niche product. You want people to associate you with a particular subject/style that way you will build an audience a following. You want people to see a picture and immediately recognise it as one of yours

Practice makes perfect.

It's a good idea to carry a sketch book with you wherever you go, to jot down ideas, sketch what you see and just have there for practice. The best way to improve your art is to just keep doing it. Sites like YouTube are fantastic for hints tips and techniques. Many artists also run Patreon pages where you can follow along on real time tutorials, these are an invaluable way to up your game. I follow 3-4 influential artists for my niche, having a role model/mentor is the best way to ensure your continued improvement. The following photos show how my work has progressed, there is 4 years between the first and 3rd drawings.

Push yourself to make every piece better than the last one. Practice wherever and whenever you can.

Notes.....

Your Niche

Task 2

Identifying Your Niche		
What is your favourite subject?		
What is your preferred medium?		
Do you like to follow a photo or create from imagination?		
Where do you see your work? By thinking where you would like to see your work, helps to identify who will see it		
Galleries		
Homes		
Parks		
Other		

Your Art Your Business

If you don't make a profit from your art, you have a hobby not a business. It is worth taking note here that although art is your passion and you feel you can not live without creating  turning it into a business may, and I emphasise MAY take a little of the joy out of what you do.

That is because running an art business is not just about creating unless you have an abundance of wealth or useful friends with varied skills there will always be aspects of your business that you don't enjoy.

The place to begin is with your mind.

You need to see what you do as WORK, don't panic, if you have been in the rat race for years the word WORK, can bring about negative feelings. We are going to change this.

If you find a job you love, you will never work a day in your life.

-Confucius

That said, you can't just float through the day doing a doodle here and commission there. You need to establish a timetable. Decide the hours that you want to work, these are entirely up to you, keep in mind when you are at your best, time when you have peace and space to create.

Set times do to set tasks. My working day is still very much 9-5pm as I have a family and pets who have their needs. Between the hours of 8-5pm I am very much alone in my studio (living room). You maybe wondering why I work from my living room, well when I first started, I would draw whenever I had a moment to spare, I was also aware that I had a full-time job as did my husband and the kids were at school. If I had set up an office or studio space in another area of the house, I would have never seen my family. Life is all about balance, they were happy for me to draw as they could still see me, talk to me and just be with me. This worked well as I never felt as though I had to choose between art and family. Also, as my house in empty in the daytime, my living room becomes my studio/office.

I will offer some insight into my general working week this is to give you an idea off what goes into running an art business you may be surprised that its not all art.

Monday

I start my week by sitting at the desk (not easel) and going through the orders, requests, invoices etc all the paperwork that has come in over the weekend, I do respond to requests as they come in over a weekend but I do not do the paperwork until my working hours (keep that balance). Some of you may relish working 24/7 and that is fine we all do what suits us and our needs.

I pair up orders with picture, print requests, invoices to suppliers etc.

I send out invoices to anybody who wishes to order and match up any photos with commission requests.

I make a list of all the commissions that I wish to work on that week, some people like to work on one piece at a time, I have a frantic head and like to switch between pieces as the mood takes.

I then sketch out the line drawings/drafts of the work that I am going to do.

I may, depending on time start on a piece of work.

Tuesday

This is a dedicated drawing day, I like to set a whole day aside to create, as after all this is my passion. When I know I have a whole uninterrupted day, I lock the doors, put the phone on Do Not Disturb, have my music loud enough to drown out distractions and just lose myself in my art

Wednesday

POST POST POST

Today I will package and post any orders completed, prints and merchandise. I am old fashioned I like to take my orders to the post office chat to the staff and build up a rapport, this can be useful when taking in large amounts of post. Keep your post workers sweet and they will be happy to sit putting recorded delivery stickers on your 50 parcels whilst chatting about their brothers, sisters. uncles wedding. Etc. Also, a box of chocolates on occasion goes a long way.

After the mothers meeting in the post office its time to Market my work.

I predominantly market on social platforms so this time is spent setting up posts, creating videos from recorded works and researching different platforms and forums. I search for any local community events where I may exhibit my work and I may come up with competitions or offers to promote. Most social media platforms have a setting where you can schedule your posts this way you can sit for a couple of hours and create many adverts to be posted out at specific times.   This means that you can hit your target market at times they are online without it encroaching into your family/relaxing time.

Thursday

Draw, paint, create.   I take this day to crack on with commissions, each piece takes approx. 10-20 hours, I like to complete at least 2-3 pieces a week. When you are deciding on your pricing which we will talk about in a later chapter; you need to figure out how much you need to make, how many pieces you will need to sell in what timescale.

This will be different for everyone and that is okay. You do need to make sure that you are keeping up with your orders to allow you to be successful in business. This is where you need to treat your art as business. It is no use saying oh I don't feel like it today I'll do it later. This is your job and you must put in the time and the hours needed.

Friday (Funday)

I run a Patreon channel (another source of income). On my channel I like to show how I create pieces of work. As with many artists we are passionate about what we do and like to guide others so they can see the beauty in art and the wonderful benefits it has for the mind. For this reason, I created my Patreon Channel. As wonderful as it is it is extremely time consuming. Creating a video with narrative takes time and patience. And lots of weird bendy arms to keep cameras, microphones etc in place.

During this time, I can either showcase a commission I am working on or take the opportunity to create something new. It is during this time that I created my 'Rainbow Hearts Series'.

If you are just starting out selling your art then you maybe creating whilst still working another job, use the same mindset and schedule time that is specifically for your art, see it as a part time business. Make sure all around you are aware of what time you wish to **spend on your art if you don't spend the time now you will never find the time to make the switch to an art career.**

Whenever you have free time and you're not drawing, take time to find inspiration and inspirational teachers, make the time to expand your skills. You should never stop learning and improving. Find out what you like and just as importantly what you don't like.

I in no way expect you to follow the same schedule as me, the purpose was to show that to make your art business successful you have to see it as that, a business, not a hobby. You can do your housework, shopping, visiting friends and family out of your working hours.

Make clear to your family and friends that although you are at home you are at work and are not to be disturbed; Just as if you were in an external office.

By setting yourself hours you will allow yourself the free time needed to get on with everything else that life brings without feeling as though it is cutting into your 'art' time.

That isn't to say if you have free time outside your working hours, you can't create. It just allows you the headspace to rest.

Work through the following task to help you plan your work, planning your week and what you need to do, want to do will help your mindset to shift from drawing for fun to drawing for profit. It will help you to identify how many hours you have and thus helping to price your art accordingly to make a living.

Task 3

Make Art your Business		
What hours do I want to work?		
What aspects of the business do I need more practice at?		
Name 3 people that can help you		
What social media platform will I use? How many times a week will I post? (3 times a week is recommended)		
Will I offer shipping? What company will I use?		
How many pieces can I produce in a typical week?		

Notes....

Marketing

Where, what, and how to sell

Marketing your art is less about promoting your work and more about promoting yourself, this may sound a little daunting at first, I am not suggesting you need to have model looks and Instagram worthy selfies to make money. What I am saying is when selling a picture, a potential buyer doesn't just fall in love with the picture they fall in love with the story.

In the early days of your art journey, you may find that you say yes to every request to draw, whether your motives are money or practice you need to be a little picky here. Some photos are just not good enough for you to pick out details or subjects that don't necessarily show of your best talents, may I suggest here that you be conscious of what you are putting out there. People will always remember the 'bad' one, it's just human nature, so make sure you showcase your best pieces.

The first thing you do is practice your picture taking skills or recruit a talented photographer friend if you have one. A fantastic piece of art can be ruined by bad lighting. Humans are very visual people but we are bombarded by images with tv and the internet, today is a generation of scrolling, your piece needs to 'catch the eye'. To do this you need a good quality photo of your piece and remember being careful is if you are photographing a piece of framed art, glass is reflective so please make sure are dressed when taking these. ….

Promoting your work on social media is the main method for artists to showcase their work in this day and age, many items are now purchased online, people spend more time looking and shopping online than ever before. If you want to sell you need to become social media savvy, there are courses and classes at many local colleges on social media studies, there are online 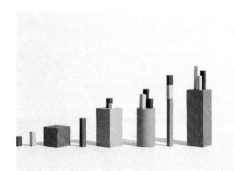 tutors and courses you can take, the best way to learn is to have a go, open an account and just play around until you feel ready.

Set yourself a 'business' account, do not your personal account to show your pieces, although many of your followers will enjoy reading about different aspects of your life, limit these only posts that relate to your art. Keep your posts professional, a potential customer wants to feel as though they are purchasing from a professional artist, they are not interested in how many shots or pints you did last night, or what you had for your lunch.

How you conduct yourself and promote your work is part of your branding no matter how you live or run your life your business page should always show the 'best' of yourself a portrait of how you see yourself as an artist.

With every piece that you post make sure that you add story, if you are posting your recent commission make sure you have the permission of the customer to post on your social media page, although as the artist you always own the rights to your art work posting an image of a portrait that is a gift for your customers friends surprise present only to be seen in advance on your page could result in a very angry customer and loss of sale.

The purpose of social media when starting out is to get your work seen and your name remembered. You need to post at least 4-5 times a week, this maybe just a picture of your recent work, or a work in progress. You may feel like you are spamming your friends but you are trying to establish your business so get yourself seen.

Get people involved in your posts, ask questions such as which is your favourite? Or what shall I draw next. This will help to bring traffic to your page.

Depending on your budget you often get the opportunity to boost your post or create an ad. From personal experience these have worked well as they send your post to people who may not normally see them, it is always worth adding 'please share' on your posts because the wider the audience the more chance you have of making a sale. Run short ads to begin with to trial what audience you get and how many sales.

With every post remember to add a next step, a next step is a way to direct people where to order or where to buy, add a link to your shop page, or instruct them to message you for more details. Make it as easy for them to buy as possible.

Website

It is imperative that you have a website, having a site to direct people too when they ask what you do shows professionalism and will make you feel like an artist.

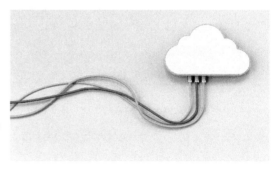

There are many companies offering free websites to begin with you can just use your site as your gallery to show off your work.

Now is the time to do a little thinking and writing work, you need to write a Bio or About Me section. Let people know who you are and why you do what you do. Tell them your passion and purpose your hobbies and an insight, where you are from and what drives you. Potential customers will purchase more freely and with confidence if they connect with you in some way.

For a small monthly fee most websites offer the option of setting up a shop, this saves so much time if selling prints or merchandise, customers can just click a link and pay, you will receive an order which will already have their contact details, payment details and requirements without a lot of to and fro with messages (the downfall of social media lots of messages back and forth for info that never results in a sale) .

Sites like Squarespace, WordPress and Wix offer free to low cast options for professional looking websites.

If this is something beyond your capabilities outsource to a company, use the help provided by the sites themselves or ask a friendly teenager.

Before advertising your website get a few friends or family to test out ease of use through multiple devices get feedback on what to improve or add before publishing it to the general public.

REMEMBER, it doesn't have to be perfect, you could procrastinate for months tweaking here and altering there, and in all that time you could have had your site 'out there' generating views and possible orders.

You can alter and mess about with the details, layout etc anytime so tweak as you go but get yourself out there for people to see. They cannot buy from you if they can't see you.

Task 4

Marketing	
What platforms will I use?	
What actions do I need to take to use the above platforms?	
How many times a week will I post	
What days/times will I set aside for this?	
What next steps can I take? (Learn new platforms, research craft fairs, selling pages etc)	
What results did I get from my last post?	
What can I change on my next post to get more eyes on my work?	
Did I put a link to order on all my posts?	

Notes….

PRICING

If you are like the majority of my art friends/clients this will be the chapter that you wanted to read most. For this I apologise because I am not going to give you a price per

size/materials etc. I am going to give you the knowledge on how to price for yourself, and explain some fantastic artists are broke.

Pricing your art has nothing to do with the materials, the quality of your work, the size or the subject. Look at Van Gogh v's Banksy for instance. And no, you do not need to be famous either.

Pricing is literally 'all in YOUR head' YOU decide what your art is worth and often we are our own worse critics so the prices will forever remain too low.

This is the most important Mindset chapter. You need to get your head around realising your value, your worth.

To start off, have a look around, find artist work that is similar in style, medium and level of your own. Have a look at their prices. How do they make you feel? Do you think you could never charge that? Is so, it's time to sort out that head of yours.

In my first year I must have altered my pricing a dozen times, because I saw other peoples work that I considered better for less money, then it was apparent I was practically working for zero cost. Before you decide how much decide on why are you selling your art? If it is purely for pleasure, friends and family then the price tag doesn't hold too much value with you.   If, however you want to make a living then you need to price you work high enough to put food on the table.

To work out a good price for your piece, identify what size, see what others in your field are charging and put the price similar to theirs Identify how this makes you feel? This is the most important factor in selling your work, YOU have to be happy with the price tag.

If you think that you are over charging you will be reluctant to tell the customer the price or be tempted to lower it or discount it. If it is too low then you will feel like you are drawing for nothing as although we all love to create, if you are working on commissions and you don't feel as though your price values your effort then your work will not be as good.

Pick a price and practice telling people how much it is. See how you feel. Find a 'happy' price. When you have picked a price, you need to be honest with yourself and break it down into price per hour and deduct your materials cost.   Make sure you are left with profit.

Making your prices too low, undervalues you, your work and other artists out there, remember you are a professional at what you do, you have put hours of time, sweat and tears into your passion, although many artists are talented this has not come without hours and hours of practice. People are not just paying for that one single piece of art they are paying for your expertise and all those hours spent getting you to this point.

Does an electrician, plumber, or architect work for minimum wage? I don't think so, you pay for their expertise and you must take into account all those hours you have put in to get you too the place where you can sell your art.

You will inevitably get people telling you that you are too expensive or that you won't sell your work for that much, that you should give your work away for free. Well, the simple thing to say in this situation is 'Thank you' and move on. These people are not your ideal clients, they are not the customers that you want buying your work. Let me have their opinion and move on.

Think, who is your ideal client, how much money do they make and what is their idea of expensive? You need to do a little work on your own mindset here, remember that what you think or feel is expensive could be considered cheap by the person next to you.

Whatever price you put on your work you will always get people on either end of the scale.

Dealing with being Ghosted.

I remember when I first started to sell my art, these were graphite pencil horse portraits, I used to sell A4 originals for £10 mainly on Facebook. They took me hours but because I was just

starting and still learning this was fine and I was happy with the extra pennies. It wasn't long before I could see a huge improvement in my skill level (drawing in your every waking moment has this effect, who knew?). I was starting to invest in courses to improve my art, better materials, mediums, art desk, lighting etc the list goes on and on, and believe me no matter what level you are at that list never seems to get any smaller.

Anyway, where was I, oh yes, so £10 per portrait was not making me any sort of profit at all, So I increased my prices very gradually. I got to my own pricing limit (an amount that I was comfortable with for the hours I put in).

This is where you start to doubt yourself, when you are at your upper price limit and someone asks for your price and then ignores you, you will be tempted to lower your prices again, offer a discount etc. Just hold on.

There are hundreds of people out there that will ask you for a price, I remember I used to get excited when anyone asked me how much? I used to see every request as a sale and then be oh so disappointed when they ghosted me. An important lesson to learn here is to not be attached to every request. Some people just want to know your prices out of interest, some are artists trying to get an insight for their pricing and some do want to know for a future purchase.   The best way to detach yourself is:

1) Have a price list ready to send
2) Have an automated response to pricing requests
3) Send your details, send one follow up a couple of days later to see if they are interested
4) Just sit back and wait for the order.

If they order great, if not they have the information they need when they are ready, they will contact you.

A big deciding factor in your pricing is what do you want the money for? For some it is extra cash from a hobby but I am guessing by the fact that you have purchased this book you want your art to pay your living expenses. This is a huge factor in your pricing.

For this you need to know how much you need to make to cover all your living expenses with enough left over for luxuries (art materials don't count, this is your business they are now necessities).

You need to work out your finances, how much do you need to make? How many pieces of art would you need to sell to make this amount?

You only have 24 hours in a day and 7 days in a week. Work out how many pieces you can produce in a week and then price to cover your expenses. If you feel that this is too much or you cannot possibly produce the amount of art you need then you need to read the next chapter on how to bring in extra income.

Pricing is individual if you are happy with your prices then they are correct for you, it is your work and your business. You are worth it and so is your art.

Task 5

Pricing		
What are my initial pricing thoughts? How much what size?		
What are the prices of my peers for the same size piece?		
How do I feel about putting my prices up?		
What scares me about putting my prices up?		
How much do I need a month?		
How many pieces at my current price would I need to produce?		
What other income streams can I create?		

Notes….

Multiple Income Streams

Sometimes our art pieces alone cannot cover all the expenses of daily living, but there is no need to be a starving artist. What you need to do is generate multiple income streams, these will bring in money when your art is not selling so fast. Multiple income streams can come in many forms. One of the easiest is to produce prints, your work is always your own, you own the copyright to all the pieces you produce therefore you can produce prints to sell. You can sell these in shops, at craft fairs or online.

Set yourself up an online shop, you can sell via, Etsy, Amazon, NOA, not on the high street, to name a few or you can sell directly from

your website or Facebook page. Prints are a fantastic way to get your art out there without having to put in the hours to create original drawings.

You can either print at home, send away to be printed or use a print on demand service where they print, package and send direct to your customers. I would suggest here that you shop around a little. Get multiple samples of your art in all different types of paper, they all vary in cost so make sure you price up costs before putting a price on your prints.

Merchandise

There are hundreds of companies out there ready to print your work onto anything you can imagine, cups, bottles, keyrings, coasters etc. as above shop around gets samples to see what you like. I have been lucky enough to have found two local ladies in my own town that produce mugs and prints. Just be careful you don't over order at first as you will be so excited to see your art on merchandise, I

know I did, but this is why I am writing this book so you can learn what not to do.

Teaching

Can you teach, can you pass on your skills to others. You can set up a local community art club or offer one to one lesson from your home or in their home. The most popular methods of teaching art are online. This does not need to be difficult when starting out you can video lessons on your phone and uploads to sites like YouTube. If you really feel this is an option for you check out the website Patreon, you may already use this to follow artists you admire, so why not you. Don't forget everyone starts somewhere and I am sure if you find early videos of your idols they won't look half as polished as they do now. You will improve with practice and time. You may just be the artist that someone is looking for to help them learn to create. Patreon is a monthly subscription service and can have multiple subscribers, it can be very time consuming so make sure you enjoy it. You can upload as much or as little content as you like. You can also offer different tiers of subscription.

Write a Book

Trust me, if I have done it so can you. I bet there is something that you really want to tell people, show the, how you do something or give advice. You can create simple step by step picture books to teach people how to create. We all do things in different ways and your way may just be what someone else is looking for.

You can produce a book with all of your artwork, a story book of your art journey.

Your biography on they why and how you became an artist.

Books are the best form of income as they are known as a passive income which basically means you can make money in your sleep. I mean is there any batter way of making money.

We all do things differently and we have all travelled different paths, what you know and where your journey has led you could be just what someone else wants to hear right now.

The thought of writing a book is scarier than the process. If you think to yourself I have to write a book, fear of the unknown will kick in and you will never get started, think instead today I will write 3 sentences on (choose whatever subject feels right at the time), and just put pen to paper or finger to keypad, before you know it, you have words on paper and you have started to write a book. Its that simple, we humans seem to over think and over complicate everything.

Want to know how to write and publish a book, this will be addressed in my upcoming webinar/course that will be available early 2022. Watch this space www.kerrispawtraits.com

See what I did there, shamelessly promoting a future course, another form of income, I am passionate about helping people to get started and if you have a passion to help, then get out there and help, there are many ways you can pass on your skills and talents.

Notes....

Task 6

Making money in your sleep	
What else can I do other than create art?	
What are my strengths?	
What are my weaknesses?	
How can I improve my weaknesses?	
Research local printers. Make a list of what products you could sell.	
Who do I know that can help me? As around friends and family, you'll be surprised what skills some people have.	

Customers Matter

Obvious really, they pay our bills, but they are far more than an income stream.

What is the best source of marketing, what can get your name out there without it costing you a penny? WORD OF MOUTH, word of mouth has always been the best form of marketing. The only way that you are going to get your customers talking about you to their friends is if you provide. Provide the best possible service that you can.

Let's start this relationship at the beginning.

The initial enquiry, you've passed over your price list and terms and conditions and they respond wanting to place an order this is where the relationship begins. This is where you become fully available to them. You are now going to become their best friend so they feel secure in dealing with you. Never forget that this a risky purchase for them, it is not like they are walking into Sainsburys picking up some bananas and handing over money. Here they literally have no idea what the finished product is going to look like and thanks to so many internet scams, rip off merchants and fake accounts, buying anything over the internet/phone carries risks. You need to help put their mind at ease.

Friendly, yes, professional definitely, the majority of customers I deal with contact me via email/messages and messenger although the conversations are very relaxed and friendly I always, ALWAYS answer messages with correct spelling and punctuation. You are your business and you want people to respect your art so act accordingly. The first thing you will need from them is a brief or photograph of what they want. This is where you need to ask a multitude of questions or request photographs. You need to know exactly what is required.

If you are working from a photograph, clearly state that you need a 'good' quality photo to work from. If your client wants any sort of portrait, that means they want a true likeness, you can only do this if you can pick out the details of a photography. The more practice you get yes, the more you can fill in details from memory of other similar subjects but this will not guarantee it will be a true likeness. Don't be afraid to tell a client that the photo is not good enough. I have put in the leg work here for you all, trust me it is far easier to have a discussion about the suitability of a photograph than it is hearing that they don't like the finished product.

Good Photo reference

Bad Photo reference

When all said and done its your work that you are putting out there, producing a substandard piece of art because of the quality of a photograph will do nothing for your portfolio, you won't want to show the piece off on social media and you may have an unhappy client. I have been there and done that too many times to mention. When I was starting out, I was excited for any sale so I would literally 'have a go' at anything. Only to disappoint myself with the results.

Stand your ground and tell them that the photo is not good enough, or if you can tell them, you can use that pose but you need better quality reference photos for the details. It does nothing for your reputation to produce substandard work. The only time I will take on a questionable photograph portrait is if the subject is deceased and this is the only photo they have. I then explain that I will do my best.

I keep customers informed throughout the whole process and send work in progress shot if they want them, that way if they are unhappy with something they can tell you before you go too far to rectify. Make sure that your customers are clear that once you are so far into your piece it cannot be changed. Otherwise you could be there forever changing the tiniest of details.

Remember to always ask if you are able to show your work in progress and the finished article on your social media for marketing purposes. The majority of the time portraits are a gift. If this is the case ask for a date that they are handing over and confirmation that you can post.   This is the main way we generate more business posting our pieces online so be clear and get the permission the last thing you want is to post a piece that ruins somebody's birthday surprise,

Posting and packaging, trust me when I say you get what you pay for. There is no point in spending hours and hours creating a beautiful piece of art, then putting it in substandard packaging for it to arrive damaged. I personally don't post my work out framed, I have tried many ways of packaging and posting from boarded envelopes to cardboard tubes. The carboard tubes are a great way to post out larger pieces of work as they are safe and secure.   My preferred method of packaging is to send the piece in a mount, this way when they arrive, they already look beautifully presented, the mount provides a hardboard to protect your work and they are ready to drop straight into a frame.

I always dress my packaging with a bit of ribbon and enclose a flyer, a business card and certificate of authenticity. Why? Because it looks professional and it show that you care about your work and its presentation.

I sometimes enclose a money off voucher too, this way they are more inclined to purchase a second piece.

Do your research and price up the many different methods and companies to ship your products. When I was starting out money was tight so shipping costs were kept to a minimum, however as I said earlier you get what you pay for. Missing artwork was frequent, for my cheaper pieces I send recorded and for the more expensive I send tracked. A little not here always remember to add a return address and as told by a lady at the post office include an invoice because anything that doesn't make it to its destination for whatever reason will be incinerated if the value is under £500. Yes this has happened to one of my pieces. You live and learn as they say.

Send your customer the tracking information, they will be very excited for their purchase to arrive, I always request that they let me know when it has arrived (although I can track it myself), this way you can check in to see if they are happy and at this point politely ask of, they can leave a review on your website/page.

Remember make sure you keep a log of all your customers and their email addresses, these will be useful to build up a customer base, many customers will order more than one piece if they are happy. You have their address so remember special occasions such as Christmas time you can send a card, and a reminder of your work any offers etc. Keep in touch customers are your best marketing team.

Notes...

SO, WHAT NOW

- **So, know you know how, get creating and enjoy every moment**
- **Celebrate every success. Dance around the room scream and shout about your achievements because YOU ARE AN ARTIST**
- **Every fail is a chance to learn**
- **Set yourself up for success, it's your art, it's your business.**
- **I know you can do this**

Thank you for purchasing Making Art your Business,

If you enjoyed this book, please leave a review and follow my website for updates on 'Making Art your business' webinar/ coaching course coming in the New year. Combining tried and tested results with a positive mindset to build your art business. Live your life to its fullest doing what you love.

Copyright Notice

I love and thank you all for supporting me in my journey and I hope I can help and support you all.

Kerri

Notes……….

Use these pages to mind dump, write down anything that comes to mind, anything that will help you on your way to creating financial freedom with your art.

Notes………

Homework

On the following pages you will find a template to map out your five year plan, why is this important? It is important because it will provide you with clarity and focus as you travel along your journey.   It will allow you to check on yourself to see if you have achieved your goals. Take each day/month/year at a time. Start where you are because every step forward is a step in the right direction.

Write down you goals everyday, why you say? Or its too much work? Really is it too much work, ask yourself how much do you want this? What are you willing to do to achieve your dream?   If you believe you will succeed then you will, these exercises help you to keep your dreams at the forefront of your mind.

"If you think you can or think you can't, you are right."

-Henry Ford

My Five Year Plan

Where do I see myself in five years time?

What can I do right now to help me get there?

What is my first task?

Start date   **End Date**

Who do I know that can help me with:-

Website:

Social media content:

Who do I admire?

Name: **Website/link**

What resources do I need to start where I am?

First year goals

Second Year Goals

Third Year Goals

Forth Year Goals

Final Year Goals

These are for you only, if you need to move goals around or change them as you go then that is up to you. If you complete them all before the 5 years then fantastic but don't let yourself off the hook, just add a few more. There is always more to learn and self improvement is a for life.

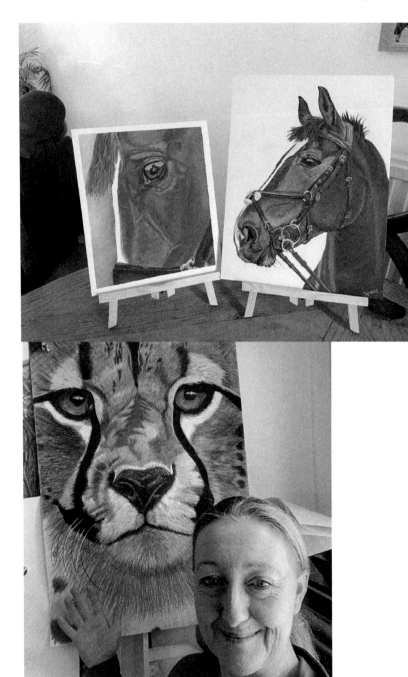

A selection of my artwork.

I started with a niche of creating horse portraits, then a natural progression to pet portraits. Although this is very time consuming the extra income freed up time for me to let the creative juices flow, I frequently play with different materials, mediums and subjects. I think commissions will always be my first love. I love working with customers and seeing their faces light up when they receive their portraits.

This book is intended as a guide to starting off a career in art, it covers the basics to get started. Keep your eyes and ears open for the next in the series taking you that one step further.

Thank you and keep creating

Kerri

Printed in Great Britain
by Amazon